CONTENTS

PANNING FOR DOGECOIN

By: Larry Turner

I f you haven't tried your luck at buying and selling cryptocurrency this is a simple method to use and be successful. It doesn't matter if you don't have much money to get started. There's money to be made even for small investments. Dogecoin is still ripe for profit. As of this writing it is about eight cents a coin. That means you can buy a thousand coins for around eighty bucks. I started with 3000; started buying and selling about a thousand at a time. The method I'm presenting has taken me to larger trades and larger profits. I know you're itching to know my method, so let's get started!

INTRODUCTION

I n 1971 NASDAQ launched its computerized, over-the-counter online trading which opened the market for just about anyone. About fourteen years later NASDAQ created the Small Order Execution System (SOES). Since then, there have been numerous online brokerage firms available for traders to simply sit at home in front of their laptops while buying and selling.

This created a new breed of traders called "Day Traders". A day trader is someone who buys and sells stocks usually on the same day. Most investors are in their portfolios for the long haul, hoping their investments will give a nice return over a long period of time; these are called long positions.

Most brokerage firms require Day Traders to maintain a minimum balance in their accounts of $ 25,000. If you're not able to do that it makes it very difficult to take advantage of this method. However, I have good news for anyone wanting to get into the cryptocurrency frenzy. Day Trading rules do not apply! Anyone can Day Trade crypto without being marked as a Day Trader and keep your brokerage account in good standing with the SEC.

I'm sure you've heard of Bitcoin's enormous rise in value over the past few years. Some folks have become very, very rich as a result. Last time I looked, Bitcoin was worth about $38,000,00 a coin.

Online brokerage firms now allow fractional shares of positions, which means you could still invest in Bitcoin with any amount of money. However, there's not much room for a huge increase in your investment. On the other hand, Dogecoin has huge possibilities for those who want to get in cheap and hope for a rally like Bitcoin. I'll explain how to do this step by step in plain, easy to understand words, without all the complicated theories and analysis used by so many high end investors.

The first thing to do is open an online brokerage account. This is easy to do. I use Robinhood and I highly recommend their platform. At present, if using this link to get started they'll give you a free share in one of many popular companies listed on the market.

https://join.robinhood.com/larryt185

Once your online account is established the next step will be to link a bank account where you can deposit or withdraw funds. You should be able to start with any amount you can afford to take off your current budget. And, if you carefully read the instructions I'm about to give you, you'll be able to steadily increase your balance on a daily basis.

Be warned, though. Don't try this on common stocks in the market unless you have a minimum balance of $25,000.00 in your account or you'll be marked as a Day Trader and be required to have that balance before doing any more trading.

Before we get started let's talk a little about cryptocurrency. This new monetary system is a digital, fiat type currency. Coins are mined by high tech equipment through a blockchain technology. It is becoming more and more popular for the international market place, and more and more businesses worldwide are beginning to utilize it in their everyday transactions. It could conceivably replace our current monetary system.

Dogecoin mining was actually started as a joke of sorts at a time when the idea of cryptocurrency was still in a speculative phase. It has gained many followers in the past few years and currently has a market cap near ten billion dollars. It is ranked pretty high of all cryptocurrency. That's saying a lot for Dogecoin since it was not meant to even be a contender at its conception. As I looked at the market this morning it was trading at $.0747 a coin.

That comes to about $74.70 for a thousand coins. If you bought a thousand coins at this price and it were to jump to $1.00 a coin you would have an investment value of $1000.00!

$1.00 a coin is but a fraction of what other coins like Bitcoin and Ethereum have managed to acquire. It's not a far fetched idea that Dogecoin could become the next big thing. According to some well known CEO's of large companies, it could very well become the "people's coin" of choice. One of them recently said that if he were given the choice of buying a lottery ticket or Dogecoin he'd definitely put his money on Dogecoin.

PANNING FOR DOGECOIN

There was a time in the not too distant past when currency was backed by a commodity like gold or silver. Every paper currency printed could be exchanged for its value in the commodity it was backed by. Today's monetary system uses fiat money which is not backed by a commodity. Central banks have control over how much money is in circulation and more control over the economy and inflation.

Crypto currency borrows its terminology from the idea of how commodities like gold were put into the market. As we all know, to get gold or silver it has to be mined from the earth by large mining companies. With cryptocurrency the mining is done in a blockchain on the world wide web. Miners use expensive equipment to find coins. With gold, individuals were able to set up small operations by panning for it. This involved using a small pan to basically sift through river beds for small amounts of gold nuggets and/or dust.

We don't have to invest in all the expensive equipment to mine our cryptocurrency. We can simply go to our brokerage account and buy or sell with no hassle. The title of this book was the result of that comparison.

DEDICATED WORK TIME

It's not practical to sit in front of your computer all day long buying and selling stocks. After all, I'm sure you'll have many other things that need to be done during your day. Fortunately for me, I am retired and this makes choosing my trading time a little easier. But, for those of you who work a regular day job there is some good news. There are two main factors that influence the buying and selling of Dogecoin. Social media and market volatility. In social media there have been some remarkable influences on Dogecoin. You get the right person to post something positive and it can bring the value up a considerable amount. One tweet on Twitter recently drove the value up about forty percent in a short time. And all that was posted was the one word, "Doge".

These social media influences can actually happen anytime, but I've noticed they're usually later in the evening. So, if you want to take a bit of your evening to do some trading the best time to do so would be from around eight p.m. eastern time, USA, to around two a.m. eastern time, USA. This time period would give you six hours to do your trading. And, while others are searching around for social media influences your busy making money as they happen live. There's really no need to try and keep up with who says what because if you're trading during those hours you're going to see the influences live on the chart and be able to take advantage of them.

Market volatility can be a book in itself, but for our purposes let's just call it a busy or slow day on the market. Market activity has a great influence on all stocks. Crypto is not left out. That's why it's good to have some specific indicators listed on your watch list that will let you know the trend.

You'll definitely want to add Dogecoin to your watch list. The reason for that is that there will be times when you may not own any Dogecoin, therefore, it will not be handy to get to on your screen. You'll have to go search for it again. On Robinhood, your watch list is always handy on the right hand side of your screen where your positions are always listed. This may not seem like a big deal, but every second counts when your trying to make the best buy or sell.

The New York Stock Exchange is open from 9:30 a.m., Eastern, to 4:00 p.m., Eastern, Monday through Friday. It will be closed on just about every holiday. Pre-market trading on Robinhood starts at 9:00 a.m.

Now, some good news for us! The Crypto markets never close. We can buy and sell 24/7.

That creates an ideal situation for the early bird, like myself. I'm usually up around three o'clock in the morning getting that first cup of coffee. Then I kick back in front of my laptop, coffee in hand, and begin my day. It's a quiet time of day, and it usually a prime time for market volatility.

Although early morning is my dedicated work time, I will still pop in and out a few times during the day just check on things and see how trading is going. If the coins are flying, I'll join the fun for a while.

LOCATING YOUR DOGECOIN

All my references are made using my brokerage account. If you have an account with a different brokerage the references I use may vary just a bit from your account, but should be easily figured out just by familiarizing yourself with the screen layout of your particular brokerage account.

In your brokerage account there should be a tab or option that displays your portfolio. Of course it will initially be empty but as you add positions to your account they will be listed in your portfolio.

On my portfolio screen there is a chart that keeps track of my portfolio value. It is a line chart that rises and falls with the value of my portfolio. Off to the side is a box that contains lists of my current positions, their current value, and how many I own. Below that is a list of other stocks I'm watching so I have easy access to them.

Below the chart is a set of icons for various other popular lists of stocks, ie: most popular, daily movers, cryptos, cannabis, pharma, energy, tech and several others.

If I click on the crypto icon it will take me to another screen with the list of crypto currencies available to view.

Along with Dogecoin there are several other cryptocurrencies listed here. For our purpose we are only interested in Dogecoin. So, I click on the Dogecoin icon. If you're using a different brokerage and Dogecoin is not listed you will have to change accounts to a brokerage that list Dogecoin.

The Dogecoin screen looks a lot like my portfolio screen. There is a line chart that keeps track of the rise and fall of the value. There is a rolling counter at the top that keeps up with the value in digital format. Just below that is a line that lists the current gain or loss in USD and percentage which is calculated from the beginning price for whichever category you're viewing.

Just below the chart is a set of tabs that let you view the chart live, for the whole day, for the week, for a month, or for several months or years of trading.

Below those tabs there are a couple of more boxes that lists my current equity, return, the average cost of one coin, and how many coins I own. This information contained in these two boxes is of the utmost concern for what we are doing. So, familiarize yourself with easy entry so you can easily refer to them once you start buying and selling.

On the right side of my chart is a box that I'll use for buying and selling. At the top of this box are two tabs: BUY DOGE and SELL DOGE. To get started we'll want to click on the BUY DOGE tab if it's not already on it.

Below those two tabs is another that lets you select whether you're buying in USD or in DOGE. For our method we will be using the DOGE option.

Below that tab is a line that shows the estimated cost of each Dogecoin you're buying.

Just under that tab is another showing the estimated cost of your buy.

Below that is a tab for reviewing your order to buy or sell.

Once this tab is selected it will show another tab to confirm the buy or sell. Once this tab is selected there is no going back. The transaction will be processed and all the details of the transaction will be stated: how much you bought, how much it cost etc.

Once again, all these are very crucial in carrying out the method we are using to make our profits, so familiarize yourself with these very well. Executing your buys and sells in a timely manner is paramount to making a profit.

ANALYZING THE CHART

Now that you have Dogecoin located let's analyze the chart a little and decide where we want to start our first buy.

You'll notice the chart has some peaks and valleys as it progresses through the time frame. These ups and downs will look dramatically different depending on which chart you're looking at. For our trading purposes we'll use the live chart which will show us the last hour of trading.

If you place your cursor over the chart you'll notice that as you move it around the rolling value indicator will show you the value at any given time during the last hour. The first thing you want to do is look at all the peaks and valleys. This will show you how high the value went before it started falling again, and how low it went before it started rising again.

With these figures you can get an average of how much change is taking place. You'll also notice that there are some dramatic changes and some less dramatic. The more dramatic the chart looks the better trading will be. This is all part of the "volatility" factor.

If the chart is not so dramatic, which is rare for Dogecoin, the highs and lows will not be so far apart. You'll just be seeing a chart without much momentum and it will basically look horizontal. The chart look that is favorable for us is one that has some high peaks and low peaks with some short horizontal changes in between them. The periods of these short horizontal changes is not of much concern for what we are trying to do.

There are three numbers we need to calculate before we start trading. First the average change in highs and lows. Hopefully you're good at math and can do this in your head. If not, keep a scratch pad and calculator handy beside your computer for quick use. For demonstration, let's say our chart has six major peaks and six major valleys. The first peak is at .085216 and the following low is at .078214; the second peak is at .083651 and the following low is at .079251; the third peak is at .084532 and the following low is at .074000; the fourth peak is at .082564 and the following low is at .078521; the fifth peak is at .080214 and the following low is at .078523; the sixth peak is at .080012 and the following low is at .078421.

If you add all these peaks together you'll get .496189. Divide that by six and the average high value is .082682.

Repeating the same process for the lows will give you an average low of .077777.

Now subtract the low average from the high average and that gives you the value of.004905. This is our first number to remember.

The second number we want is the amount of momentum the chart is experiencing during the last hour of trade. Subtract the first peak from the second peak; the difference is .001565. Subtract the second peak from the third peak; the difference is .000881. Subtract the third peak from the fourth peak; the difference is .001968. Subtract the fourth peak from the fifth peak; the difference is .002350. And, subtract the fifth peak from the sixth peak; the difference is .000202.

Add all the answers together and divide by five; your second number to remember is .0013932. This number tells us the average progression of price through the hour of trading. Simply looking at the chart will tell you if the momentum is upward or downward.

If the momentum is on an upward trend, this is the ideal

situation for trading. You could still make a profit even when it is moving down but I just prefer to wait on the ups again. There are a few risky situations in the down market.

Alrighty then! Moving right along. Don't let all the numbers discourage you. It's really not that complicated. And the rewards are worth the effort! So, on to our third number to remember.

The third number is actually a time frame. Move your cursor over the peaks once again and take note of the time indicated at that peak. Do this on each one and find an average length of time it took for each peak to arrive on the chart. For demonstration purposes our peaks in this example average 5 minutes apart from each other.

SUMMARY OF CHART ANALYSIS:

Average change in value   = .005
Average rise or decrease in value = .001
Average time between trades   = 5 minutes

USING YOUR NUMBERS

Analyzing a stock chart can be a mathematical dilemma. Many highly educated individuals use chart analysis to make their trades work to their advantage. My experience has led me to use a monetary value system instead of depending so much on averages and statistics. So, to use these three numbers we've arrived at we'll need to convert them to monetary values.

Actually, doing this is not all that complicated. To get to our monetary value we just need to first decide how much we are going to start with. That amount is entirely up to you. Robinhood has no maximums on account value. So, for demonstration let's just say we're going to start our trading with a $1000.00 deposit into the account. It could in reality be any amount you can afford to start with, though. However, the more you can trade with will give you more momentum in the increase of your value.

With a thousand dollars invested at the trading value of Dogecoin, in this example, we can buy a ten thousand coins. If the current buying value is .079521 , for example, we could purchase 10,000 coins for $795.20. This first buy should be made during a low phase of the ups and downs. You wouldn't want to buy at a high phase only to watch the value of your coins drop considerably. The idea here is to buy low and sell high. Using our numbers will give us the best advantage of this process.

We own some Doge !!! Ooooh weeee! Isn't this exciting!

Now let's get some monetary value established. With ten thousand coins in our portfolio we'll have a change in value as the trading and selling progresses. Let's take a look at the value in each digit of the rolling counter on our chart. The first digit is the dimes, so to speak. For every increase in ten cents our Doge value would increase $1,000.00. The second after the decimal is the cent digit; for every increase in cents our Doge value would increase $100.00. The third digit is one tenth of a cent. For every increase our Doge value would increase by $10.00.

In our chart analysis our first number is .005. The five is in our third digit area of the counter so our average monetary change is $50.00

Our second number which is our average rise or decrease in value is .001. If our chart is going up this means that every time we trade we can expect our monetary value of the trade to increase by $10.00. Our first buy was for $795.20. So we can expect our second buy to be for about $805.20.

Our third number, the time between trades is 5 minutes. That lets us know that we can expect to be making our first sell about five minutes after the first buy.

It's fairly risky to hold these numbers to their exact value so what I do is allow for some differences. The first buy was at $795.20; my analysis says that the price will increase to $805.20 before it starts to fall again. I'm planning on selling at $800.20. My increase will be $10.00. I can make this increase every five minutes. So, I can plan on increasing my value by $60.00 dollars every hour of trading.

The key here is getting your trades in before they start a change in direction. The formulas I've given will calculate out to some very good indicators for when to click that buy or sell tab!

The method is not really all that complicated. Once you familiarize yourself with the brokerage screens and the thinking behind the math, you will be able to make your buys and sells without having to take time to do all the math.

Making money in the market is as simple as buying low and

selling high. That sounds easy enough, but without the timing it just doesn't work. Panning for Dogecoin is simply a blueprint of my thinking while I"m trying get the timing right! It works for me and it will work for you.

FINAL WORDS

I would suggest several readings of this book before taking a plunge into trading Dogecoin. In trading any stocks or commodities there are always risks involved. And there are sometimes anomalies in trading that will throw the analysis off a bit. So, it's very important to watch carefully at what's going on during your trading session. I've developed a few strategies to help me minimize these anomalies.

Most of the time I will sell in larger quantities of coins because the price is apparent and I know what I'm going to receive for the sale. I've progressed through the selling process to the very last tab, which is the submit tab. I'll watch the counter for the selling price while I'm ready to click the tab; once the price is ripe I simply click submit and the sell takes place immediately. If I'm sitting at the review stage of selling I'm risking a greater change in value by the time I get to submit. Changes can occur in fractions of a second.

Sometimes, I'll buy in smaller quantities. The reason for this is the value is in a down mode when I'm getting ready to buy and there's always the possibility that it will even decrease more after my buy. This is defeating my purpose for the buy. If it does this, I'll buy more.until the price starts to rise again. If I'm trading five thousand coins at a time my buys will probably be a thousand each and my sell will be for the entire five thousand.

I use the same technique for selling as for buying. I'm on the submit tab ready to make the sell immediately when the price peaks out.

    I use the analysis method given here to decide how much value to expect and when to execute my trades. I stick with it. Don't take any chances. If you have calculated a figure for increase, be happy with it. Even if the value goes up more after you trade. It will eventually come back down. If you try to wait out a larger increase before you sell you're taking a chance on it dropping and missing your target. Doing so would decrease your expected value or cause a loss of valuable time between peaks for your next trade.

    There will be those rare times when the price goes on a frenzy and starts to skyrocket. It would certainly be to your advantage to try and wait it out a bit if this happens. The best indicator that this might be happening is no intermediate rise and falls between trades. Looking back at the chart you can see that between our peaks and valleys there are always some slight up and down movements. If your value has risen to your expected point and there are no downward movements prior to it, it would certainly indicate a continued rise in value. Hopefully, you and I both are at the helm when Dogecoin goes to the moon!

    As a final word, thank you for reading. Of course, I have to leave a little disclaimer. There's no absolute guarantee that any system of trading will work all the time. There are always variables in any method; even mine.

    I do believe you can be successful at making money with Dogecoin. Stay alert, be smart, and don't get greedy. Be patient and determined. I can only tell you for sure it works for me.

    Good luck! Have fun! To the moon, baby !!!!!!

NOTES:

(Use these pages for figuring your three numbers)

NOTES:

(Use these pages for figuring your three numbers)

NOTES:

(Use these pages for figuring your three numbers)

NOTES:

(Use these pages for figuring your three numbers)

www.ingramcontent.com/pod-product-compliance
Lightning Source LLC
Chambersburg PA
CBHW072154230526
45467CB00042B/2150